Still Haunted

Willow Cross

DEDICATION

A special thanks to those of you who have shared your stories with me and graciously allowed me the opportunity to share them with Haunted fans. You rock!

ACKNOWLEDGMENTS

Thank you JH Glaze and MostCool Media for providing me with such awesome covers. You always seem to read my mind and know exactly what I want.

i

HAUNTED III

Forward

Unlike the previous two Haunteds, this edition does not include just my personal ghost stories. Instead, I have added stories from people I know. The first is my own; however, those that follow belong to good friends who have also encountered the paranormal.

Although I have no documented proof their claims are true, I do believe each story is an honest and truthful account of the paranormal events they endured. Each story has been written and relayed to you, the reader, in the exact manner in which it was told to me. I've added nothing for dramatic effect. All those who participated in this edition have been thoroughly interrogated, so that I could be certain nothing important was left out of the telling. All the names and locations have been changed in order to protect the identities of those involved.

Prologue

When we left the dream home and moved to Arkansas, I'd mistakenly believed myself finally free of ghostly manifestations, strange knocks, weird noises, and disappearing objects. After so many years of living with spirits I'd become quite attuned to their 'frequency' for lack of a better term. I'm not sure how to explain it in better terms, but I'll give it a go.

When I'm in a haunted location I get the normal goose bumps, feelings of dread or sorrow, and also an inexplicable feeling of surging electricity. I can't see or hear it, but it feels like the actual air around me is buzzing. The sensation is akin to the one many folks have just before the onset of a tremendous thunderstorm. The hair on the back of my neck and arms will rise and I just 'know' there's something there.

Now, being used to these sensations, I've honed this instinct into a warning system of sorts. And I've learned to utilize it when the necessity arises. Moving into a new home was just that sort of necessity.

A month before our move, we came down to look at rental properties and finalize my husband's transfer to his new job. I rented the first and only house we looked at. Of course that sounds ridiculous, but I had list and this house qualified on every item needed.

Number one on that list was: Not Haunted. Seriously.

Knowing my idiosyncrasies, my husband didn't even flinch when I asked to him get the landlord outside so I could walk the house alone. He knew what I wanted to do. As they chatted in the driveway, I walked through every room and into every last closet. In each I'd stand quietly, close my eyes, and take in the ambiance of the space, waiting for those 'sensations' to stir up. Nothing. Not one blessed goose bump. No rising hair follicles and no electricity, just a calm sense of peace.

The house was a wreck. Seriously dirty, still had the previous tenant's belongings strewn about, and in need a massive overhaul. And guess what? I wrote the landlord a check that day to secure the property. He assured me that things would be neat and tidy on move in day and that was good enough for me. I was sad to be leaving my dream home, but at the same time, elated to be free of the supernatural elements which had been disrupting my life for so many years.

The actual move was clean, quick, and relatively easy. We settled in, the kids started their new schools, and I got to know some of the neighborhood moms. I did a smidge of research on the house through my neighborhood connections and discovered that our landlord had actually built this house himself and lived in it until his children were grown. No one had ever died here and for the next several years we lived in total peace and bliss. I will never forget September of 2008. That was the month I discovered that the places I'd lived before probably had little to do with the hauntings I'd experienced.

THE BOY IN THE CLOSET

Fall was upon us and the kids were enjoying being back in school. I was little sad to put the lazy summer days behind me, but it was September, which meant we were gearing up for Halloween! Halloween and Christmas have always been big deal holidays for our family, so everyone was excited about putting out decorations and planning for our yearly Halloween celebration.

Surprisingly, I was not the first in the family to encounter our new visitor. My youngest daughter brought him to my attention. One morning, as we hustled about getting ready for school, I noticed my 13-year-old daughter standing outside her room staring at the door. Her face was pale, and she was only half dressed.

"Kerri, get the lead out. You're going to miss the bus!" I said.

Her eyes misted with tears as she turned to face me. "I can't go in there."

Shoving past her, I pushed open the door and

stomped into the room expecting to see one of her older sisters. As with most siblings, my children could be extremely mean to each other on occasion. From the look on her face I'd assumed someone had told her to get out, but the room was empty.

Sighing, I turned to her and scolded, "No one's even here. Hurry up and get dressed! I don't want to have to drive you to school this morning. Traffic is horrible this time of day."

She took a tentative step forward and peered around the room before finally stepping in. Before I could leave the room, she'd literally jumped into her jeans, crammed her feet into her shoes, and headed back out the door. About that time, her older sister rounded the corner, nearly colliding with her.

"What's wrong with your sister? Did you do something to her?" I asked.

Marie shrugged. "I have no clue, Mom. She's a weirdo."

"She's not a weirdo and you'd better stop being mean to her. And by the way, you guys share that room so stop telling her she can't be in it! The next time that happens, you're grounded."

As I walked away, she called out, "I didn't do anything to her. She's just trying to get me in trouble!"

Certain I'd taken care of the problem, I went on with my day and never gave the incident another thought until the next morning. As usual, I awoke, started my coffee brewing, and went to wake up the children. As I moved through the living room to the girls' room in the back of the house, I noticed a small bundle of blankets on the couch with mass of dark curls peeking out from underneath. Kerri was curled in a tight ball, sound asleep. "Baby, get up. It's time to get ready for school. What are you doing out here?"

She stretched, yawned, and opened her eyes.

"Answer me. Why did you sleep on the couch?"

Immediately, a fearful expression clouded her face. "I can't be in there, Mom."

I was instantly angry. "Marie!" I yelled.

"No, it's not her. She didn't do anything," Kerri pleaded.

"If she's not picking on you, then why can't you be in your own room?"

Kerri sat straight up and searched my face as if looking for some sign of something. "There's something in there."

At this point, I really should have guessed, but we'd already found a garter snake, a small lizard, and various sizes of terrifyingly hairy wolf spiders in the house, so it just didn't click. "What do you mean by *something*?"

She sighed and flashed a look of fierce determination. "A ghost, Mom. There's a ghost in my room."

Along with the entities who seem determined to make contact with me, how I responded to her will haunt me forever. I did the one thing that someone with my personal experiences should never do. "Oh for heaven's sake. There's no ghost in your room. This house is not haunted!"

"It is! There's someone in there and it won't leave me alone. It pulls my hair, and wakes me up at night. It whispers stuff to me, but I can't understand what it's saying."

I could tell by the tone of her voice she wasn't lying. Whatever was going on, she believed it to be true and was honestly scared. But I knew this house wasn't haunted. I'd been very thorough in checking it out and my ghost-dar did not go off. It couldn't be haunted!

We rushed around and thankfully, everyone got out the door on time. After they'd left, I followed my normal routine until my list of daily chores was finished and then plopped on the couch with a new book and started to read. Before too long, all I could think about was Kerri's terrified expression. What was going on with her? Was this some sort of residual effect from living in the other houses? Was she losing her mind?

I put the book down, lit some incense and starting at the back of the house, did another walk through. The 'frequency' of the house was noticeably different. Not necessarily ghostly, but still different all the same. My ghost-dar remained quiet as a church mouse all the way through the house. Until I stepped into the girls' bedroom. Now I'm not saying all the bells, whistles, and sirens went off because that would be a serious over statement. Instead, I just got this feeling of not quite rightness. Not really wrongness, but something was off kilter.

I was so aggravated. How does a ghost-free house become haunted when no one's ever died there? It didn't make sense. Here I was once again, dealing with something I had no idea what to do about. So I did the only thing I could do, I got online and began researching ghosts and hauntings, specifically looked for something that could explain what might be happening here. All the while telling myself, this house was not haunted. Not again. There was no way this was happening again.

***

The next several days passed with without so much as a hint of trouble, other than the normal trivial drama between siblings. In fact, it was so calm I managed to convince myself that Kerri's statements were simply the result of an over-active imagination. She went back to sleeping in her room, and whatever had rattled her nerves seemed to no longer be an issue.

The following Saturday night, I was awakened from a dead sleep by multiple screaming voices. Leaping from the bed, my feet slid against the carpet as they hit the floor. I don't know what I did or how I managed it. First I was falling and suddenly I was sitting on the side of my bed with my legs dangling. Maybe I'd performed some sort of awesome ninja move I didn't know I could do, but with my complete lack of graceful abilities...chances of that were slim to none. Before I could get up, all four of my girls were crowded around me in various stages of hysteria and all trying to talk at the same time.

My husband rolled over with a growl. "What the hell is going on?"

The frightened girls proceeded to get louder in their attempt to fill us in.

"All right!" I raised my voice. "That's enough. Take a breath and calm down. Renae, what happened?" I said to the oldest.

"There's someone outside! They're trying to get in!" she answered.

The other girls nodded their heads in agreement and Gail busted in with, "We heard the door knob rattle on the front door and then saw him looking in through the living room window. We thought it was one of the boys, but they're all in bed."

About that time the boys showed up in the hallway. Dale, the oldest, had already turned around and headed toward the front door. Jarod, the next oldest, was close on his heels.

While the girls chattered away, I grabbed my robe,

pushed through them, and went after the boys. Being in their late teens, they still suffered from 'superman' ideations and I was certain they were about to attempt to beat the tar out of a peeping Tom.

They were already out the door by the time I entered the living room. Stepping out on the front porch, I called out, "Boys?"

"Yeah, Mom," Dale answered as he came around the side of the house.

"You find anything?"

Laughing, he shook his head. "They're crazy. No one's out here."

Coming from the other end of the house, Jarod was also shaking his head. "Nothing here. I even looked in the shed."

We went back in the house and joined the girls in the living room. Once again they recounted their story.

Tired and seriously frustrated, I crossed my arms over my chest. "What were you guys doing up anyhow?"

"Watching movies," they answered.

"Scary movies?"

Their expressions varied from sheepish to downright offended.

"That had nothing to do with it, Mom. We saw someone!" Renae protested.

Sighing, I motioned the snickering boys back to their bedroom. "Okay, you girls hit the sack. No more scary movies this late at night. If it's going to freak you out that bad, then watch them during the day."

"But, Mom!" Kerri whimpered. "There really was someone out there!"

Pulling her into my arms, I squeezed her tight. "Honey, if there was someone out there, you guys scared him off with your screaming. He probably hung around close enough to watch and saw both of your big brothers outside. That means he knows you girls are not here alone, and would anyone in their right mind want to mess with your brothers?"

She laughed. "No. Probably not."

"Well, okay then. Bedtime. And just to be on the safe side, make sure your blinds are down and closed. Got it?"

"Yes, Ma'am," they answered in unison.

One at a time, I kissed them all on the forehead and smacked their behinds as they filed down the hall to their room at the other end of the house. After making sure all of the doors were locked, I shut off the TV and lights and plodded back to bed.

My husband groaned and rolled towards me as I crawled back in. "What was that all about?"

Irritated that he hadn't even bothered to get up and check it out for himself, I answered, "Peeping Tom. Boys took care of it."

Of course at that point he jumped right out of bed and had to go check things out himself. Several minutes later he returned with an angry expression on his face. "I didn't see anything."

"I told you the boys took care of it."

Minutes later I dozed off, but it didn't last long. Within the hour the girls were screaming again. That time it was someone knocking on their window. Once again we checked the exterior of the house and found nothing.

At that point they were too freaked out to even step into their room, so Dale and Jarod decided one would sleep in the living room and one would sleep in the girls' room. The girls? They slept in my room on the floor.

When we awoke the next day, my husband and the boys carefully checked for footprints or any sign of tampering with the windows and doors. Of course they found nothing at all. Except for the girls, the rest of us were convinced it was one of their friends playing a joke on them. It almost had to be. A stranger wouldn't know which bedroom was theirs.

We continued to laugh about it throughout the day, but late that night...it happened again. However, this time it was my window and there was no screaming to alert the culprit that we were coming after him.

I was just dozing off when I heard three very distinctive taps against my window. I sat up in bed and listened intently. Within seconds, I heard another *tap tap tap*. Not *tinks*, like the sound of small pebbles hitting the window, and it most certainly wasn't the *click* of branches bouncing off the pane. It sounded like a bare set of knuckles softly hitting the glass.

Shaking my husband awake, I motioned to the window and my ear. He nodded and listened with me. This time the taps were a little louder and closer together.

Leaving the light off, he jumped out of bed and pulled on his sweatpants. Without speaking a word, he pointed to himself and made a circling motion with his finger. I pointed to myself, the back of the house, and repeated the circling motion.

Leaving the lights off, we moved quietly through the house, each to a separate entrance.

As I disengaged the bolt lock on the back door, I jumped. It sounded so much louder than I'd thought it would. Armed with the broom I'd grabbed as I walked through the kitchen, I slipped out the door and around the side of the house toward our bedroom window. Pat was already standing there when I arrived. "Did you see anyone?" I whispered.

Looking over my shoulder, he put his finger to his lips and tilted his head toward the shed. I nodded and followed behind him. He went in the door and I went around the back.

Nothing. Everything was in its place and there was no one in sight.

Pat was beyond pissed off. Making his tone much louder than necessary, he let out a string of cuss words and said, "That's it. I'm going down to the police department tomorrow and making a report. And when we find out who's jacking around out here, they can go to jail."

"Yep!" I agreed. "And they deserve to go to jail. What if we'd come out with a gun? We could have killed them without even realizing they weren't trying to break in!"

Almost as if in response to what we'd said, an icy chill came over me causing me to shiver. I quickly looked around again, but still didn't see anything out of place. That chill stuck with me though. Even after we'd returned to the house and crawled back in bed, the coldness of a breeze that shouldn't have been there stayed on my mind. The sensation was all too familiar and I couldn't help but wonder if the prankster was a 'who' or a 'what.'

The following night I stayed up as late as I possibly could, waiting for the idiot prankster to return. Sometime after 3:00 am I gave up and fell asleep. It seemed like the moment I'd closed my eyes, it began again. This time the knocking came from inside the house. On the bathroom door just down the hall to be precise. The first three knocks easily woke me. The second set of knocks had me on my feet. And by the time the third set sounded I was already on my way to the bathroom to give whoever was knocking on the door that time of night a piece of my mind. Seriously? Why in the world would anyone in the house be knocking on the bathroom door at 3 am? No one in this entire household is that polite!

By the time the fourth set of knocks sounded I was already standing in front of the door. Alone. Without giving it half a thought, I grabbed the knob and shoved the door open, fully expecting to make contact with the body behind it. I was really shocked when it swung in without even the slightest snag. Even more so, when I saw the dark, empty room. Just to be certain no one was screwing with me, I flipped the light switch and pulled back the shower curtain. No one.

No matter how bad I wanted to believe we'd escaped the paranormal, there was no doubt in my mind that we had a ghost. Again. The strangest thing was, that unlike any of the other hauntings I'd endured, there were no feelings of fear or trepidation. I was seriously frustrated, but I just accepted it and went back to bed. My biggest concern was for the children. They didn't like it and the two youngest most certainly weren't old enough to accept that it was just a part of our lives and deal with it. Especially my youngest daughter. Every incident, even the barely perceivable events, absolutely terrified her.

The next morning everything went according to our usual schedule. I didn't say anything to anyone about my experience the night before. My plan, and I did have what I thought was a very good plan, was to get rid of it before another event could occur.

As soon as the children were gone, I jumped online and began researching ways to expel ghosts. There were literally hundreds of websites addressing the issue. One of the few things they had in common was the fact that there wasn't one particular way to be rid of the pests. What might work for one person, may not work for another. I was already a little nervous about undertaking this sort of project. I'd never felt the need to be rid of a ghost. I'd either moved, or lived with them. However, I was determined that my children wouldn't have to deal with the paranormal again, so no matter what I had to try, this ghost was leaving. End of story.

Finding the necessary accoutrements to rid myself of paranormal entities in my tiny town was ridiculously hard. Even something as simple as a bundle of sage for smudging was unattainable. So I made do with what I could find. A trip to the local grocery provided me with ground sage, vanilla extract, and white candles.

After lighting a candle in each room, I started at the back of the house and lit the ground sage. The stench was overwhelming. That stuff stunk so bad I still smelled it days later! As I walked into each room I read Saint Michael's prayer start to finish, repeating it as I entered the next space. When the entire house had been covered, I went outside and walked all the way around the property repeating what I'd just done inside. Then, just in case the situation was a bit like bombing for bugs, I went across the street to my friend's house and visited with her for a couple hours before returning home to air out the house.

By the time the kids came home from school, the house smelled of vanilla and everything seemed right as rain. I was pretty proud of myself. Time would tell for sure, but it seemed like whatever or whoever our visitor was, it was gone.

The next few weeks flew by and before we knew it, we were preparing for the Thanksgiving holiday. The children in our school system get the entire week of Thanksgiving off, so that whole week our house is overrun with not only our own children, but their friends as well.

Wednesday night I stayed awake until 1:00 am to put the turkey in the oven. I like to put it in overnight so that it's finished cooking by morning leaving the oven available for all the side dishes. After triple checking the oven temperature, I dropped by the girls' bedroom and told them it was time to sleep. They moaned and groaned as I shut off their stereo and television and waited for them to crawl in their beds. Once everyone was settled, I flipped the light off and went to my own.

As soon as I laid my head on my pillow, my body reacted the way it always does when I know I have a hectic day ahead. I was wide awake. I tried to close my eyes and relax, but it just wasn't working, so I grabbed the remote and began channel surfing. Three or four rounds through 200 plus channels didn't help me find anything to occupy my mind. Clicking the off button, I closed my eyes again and tried to visualize someplace exotic with white sandy beaches and a multitude of palm trees swaying gently in the wind.

My eyes snapped open the moment I felt the nudge against my shoulder. The bedroom was so dark I could barely make out the shape standing over me. Gasping, I sat straight up in bed. My racing heart caught in my throat as I heard, "Mom, it's me."

Exhaling heavily, I hissed, "What are you doing, Kerri? You scared me half to death!"

"There's a--"

"Shhh!" I cut her off before she could wake Pat. "Whisper."

Leaning in, she spoke softly. "You have to come here. There's a boy in my closet."

Still attempting to calm my pounding heart, I motioned to the door and then followed after her into the hallway. Pulling the bedroom door shut, I turned to face her. "What boy?"

She shrugged. "I don't know who it is. I was laying in my bed and had almost fallen asleep, when I felt someone standing over me. I opened my eyes to see who it was and it was this guy. I think I scared him. He looked shocked and then ran into my closet."

"So you are telling me there's a real person in your closet right now?"

She shook her head. "No. He's definitely not real."

"Oh, Kerri," I sighed. "I'm so tired."

Reaching out, she placed her hand on my arm. "Mom, please. Just come and look."

I shook my head, but plodded towards the girls' room, intent on making quick work of the situation and getting back to bed.

The other girls moaned when I flipped on the light. Two pulled the covers over their head, but Gail sat up and rubbed her eyes. "What's going on, Mom?"

"Apparently we have a visitor. I'm just checking things out."

Now the girls' bedroom is by far the largest room in the house. It used to be two separate rooms, but sometime before we moved in, someone had taken the wall between them out. Almost dead center of the room, off to one side, stands a large walk-in closet. Both folding doors were spread open, but the light was off.

I hit the light switch beside it and glaring florescent bulbs filled every corner of the closet. No one was there. Not that I was seriously expecting to see anyone at that point. Still standing just in front of the closet, I turned to face both Gail and Kerri. "No one is here. Everything looks perfectly normal."

Before I'd finished saying the word normal, I felt a tap against my leg. Simultaneously, both girls jumped, yelped, and stepped back. I looked down to see what had hit my leg and a white plastic hanger was lying by my foot.

"Holy crap!" Gail exhaled.

Once again I turned to face the closet. This time I walked right inside and started moving the clothes around to look behind them. Still finding nothing at all, I put my hands on my hips and said, "Okay, that's enough. I don't know who you are, or why you are here, and guess what? I don't give a rat's ass either. Stop bothering my children and get out of my house!"

My entire body shivered as goose bumps covered me. It was like an arctic blast had settled around me. I shook my head and stood my ground. "Is that all you got? You can throw a two ounce plastic hanger and give me goose bumps? Ooooo, you are so scary," I taunted.

Pausing to see if anything else would happen, I finally continued. "Seriously, dude, get out of my house. You don't belong here. We are not your family, and this is not your home. Get out! Now!"

Now I swear, and I'm sure most won't believe me, but I do have witnesses...the chilled air faded into normal room temperature and as it left I heard muffled laughter. I'm sure my eyes were as wide as saucers as I looked at the girls. "Did you hear that?"

Both nodded.

"Is it gone?" Kerri asked.

Trying my best to give her a reassuring smile, I answered, "For now. I don't think he'll bother you again tonight. As soon as I can get you all out of the house, I'll take care of him for good."

As it turned out, I never had to do anything else. He must have taken me seriously because he never showed his face, or his aptitude for hanger throwing, around our house again. Most importantly, I'd learned something. Taking control of your space, being in charge of your home, and knowing--beyond a shadow of a doubt--that you own everything in your 'space'...is a weapon you can use. An extremely valuable tool when you are dealing with some aspects of the paranormal.

THE NANNY GHOST
(ANNOYMOUS)

I've been seeing ghosts for nearly as long as I can remember. However, I didn't know they were ghosts in the beginning. I had two kinds of friends when I was a little girl. The friends my parents and family could see and the friends that only I could see. To be honest I liked my invisible friends better than the regular friends. Flesh and blood friends are only allowed to come over and play certain times of day or for some, certain days of the week. But my invisible friends could play with me any time I wished for it. Even in the middle of the night.

The first ghostly memory I have is of a young woman named Margie. She was very tall and beautiful in her flowing white gown. Her dark hair was always piled up on her head in a loose bun that allowed curled tendrils to sneak out around her face, perfectly framing her ice blue eyes.

When I think back on it now, it surprises me that I never seemed to notice how pale she was. The fact that it never seemed to bother me that I could see through at least part of her most of the time just goes to show how well children take people at face value I suppose.

I met Margie just after my fifth birthday, on the day we moved from our tiny apartment to a two-story, four bedroom house. I'd hauled my pink Care bear book bag, filled with numerous Barbies and all their accessories, all the way to the top of the stairs and there she stood, just inside the doorway to one of the empty bedrooms. Her face lit up with a smile and she waved with the excitement of someone who'd just run into an old, dearly loved friend.

The fact that she was a stranger in my new home completely eluded me. And when she spoke, any misgivings, if I'd thought to have any at all, were completely wiped away.

"Well, hello there, Little Miss. I'm Margie. What's your name?"

I grinned. Little Miss sounded like a big girl name and even though I was a big girl, no one ever seemed to notice. "Hi! I'm Cindy. Are you my new babysitter?"

She giggled infectiously and answered, "Oh, heavens no. This is my house too, but I'm going to share it with you. Would you mind living here with me?"

I shook my head. "Will you play with me?"

From somewhere downstairs, my mother yelled, "Cindy? Where are you?"

Margie put her index finger to her lips and whispered, "This has to be our secret, all right? Can you do that?"

Shoving my shoulders back, I brought my chin up proudly. "I'm a big girl. I can keep secrets."

When Mom yelled the second time, I leaned over the banister and hollered back, "I'm up here. Which room is mine?"

"The green room is for me and Daddy and I'd like to use the small blue room beside it for the nursery, but you can pick whichever you like best from the other two."

Excited with the opportunity, I quickly turned to my new friend and was surprised to find she was no longer there. Figuring she'd moved into the bedroom, I quickly followed.

It was a lovely room. The walls were covered in worn wallpaper with vines of ivy printed all over them. It sort of felt like being in a special garden. A large window faced the front of the house, letting in loads of sunlight and just beneath it was a built-in seat with a large faded green cushion.

"This is my room," I heard Margie say. Spinning, my eyes darted back and forth over every inch of the room, but I was completely alone.

"Where are you?" I asked.

Still completely invisible, she giggled and then answered. "I'm here. I'll always be here if you need. You should stay here in this room with me. Then you will never be alone."

Being someone who was afraid of the dark, and also especially frightened of storms and spiders, it sounded like a good plan to me.

The next morning I woke to mom's voice calling me down for breakfast and looked around my room hoping for a glimpse of my new friend. It was very strange the way she could come and go so quickly, but then again, it was her house first and she knew it better than I did. I hurried down to eat and just as I rounded the corner and stepped into the kitchen, I saw her. She was standing just behind Mom looking over her shoulder.

Turning to face me, Margie smiled.

***

The days flew by and soon the chill of spring gave way to the scorching heat of summer. With each passing day, our friendship grew stronger and before long, Margie was everything to me. My best friend, confidant, playtime buddy, and constant care giver. Now, she didn't make me sandwiches and lemonade, or anything of that nature, but she did have a way of making scraped knees hurt less than they should. Come to think of it, she was pretty good at making any boo boo go away fairly quickly.

My baby brother came just a few weeks after the move and mom was always occupied with diaper changing or bottle feeding, or any number of chores that had to do with little Jakie. A normal child would have probably been terribly jealous of the situation, but I wasn't normal and I had Margie.

We did everything together. We had tea parties, she'd talk to me while I played on the swing outside, and every night before I went to bed she'd tell me stories about her life. Over the course of many months she'd told me about being a little girl in our house and how her poor mother had succumbed to a sickness called small pox and died. Margie contracted it too and had died in that very room. She was very sad about it because she'd had a young man that she was supposed to marry and her wedding was just a few days off when her body finally gave in to the disease. She told me all about the wedding dress. Her father had ordered it specially made from a fancy dressmaker in a big city, and according to her, it was still up in the attic in a very old trunk.

At some point, and I honestly can't remember when, I stopped keeping our secret and talked about her incessantly. Neither Mom nor Dad believed she was real. Both referred to her as my imaginary friend. Honestly, that used to make me quite angry, but I knew better than to push the issue. Margie said if they found out she was real, they'd move and then we'd never see each other again. As young as I was, I knew she was right and I didn't want to lose my best friend.

In the fall, I went to school for the very first time. That was a real eye opener for me. I learned very quickly that most children do not have imaginary friends. Soon, I quit talking about Margie completely. Other kids don't like to play with children who see things they can't. And they are pretty mean about it too.

Halloween was approaching quickly and Mom and Dad had decided they were going to throw a costume party to celebrate the occasion. For weeks they planned the menu, made guests lists, and decorated. The week of the party I came home from school to find my mother standing in the living room over a dark brown trunk with rusty hinges. She was holding a long white gown that had been discolored in places with streaks of yellow, just under her neck.

She smiled at me and said, "What do you think? If I throw some red paint on this it will be the perfect zombie bride costume."

I was horrified. The thought of Margie's expensive wedding dress being painted to look bloody, just for a party, sent me straight to tears.

"You can't, Mom! You can't do that to Margie's dress!" I wailed.

"Well what in the world has gotten into you?" she

replied.

"That's Margie's wedding dress," I babbled. "She never even got to wear it before she died! That's her very favorite thing!"

My Mom stiffened and quickly looked around the room. "How can this be Margie's dress, dear? Children don't have wedding dresses."

Jutting my chin out in determination, I responded angrily, "She's not a kid. She's a lady. A very pretty, nice, lady. And she's my friend!"

My mother's left eyebrow rose and she gave me that looks she always gives me when she thinks I'm not telling the truth. "A lady, huh?" she said.

Crossing my arms, I glared at her defiantly. "Yes, she is. Her name is Margaret Adeline Bowman and this is her house. And she's been nice enough to let us live with her. And you can't take other people's things because that is stealing!"

My mother's face went completely white and she looked around the room again. Dropping the dress back into the trunk, she moved to the couch and motioned for me to come sit beside her. I did as she'd asked, but belligerently. I was still angry that she'd even *think* about doing something mean to Margie's dress.

Mom asked me one question after another about my friend. I told her about Margie being the only girl in a family with three boys. About how she and her mother had died from the small pox. I even told her about how Margie went looking for her boyfriend after she died and her sorrow when she couldn't find him. We talked until Jakie woke up from his nap and after that, for the rest of the day, she never said another word about Margie or the dress.

Sometime during the afternoon, the trunk and

dress disappeared from the living room. Probably while I was up in my room with Margie spilling my guts about totally giving away our secret. I was horribly afraid she'd be cross with me, but instead she just nodded and gave me that sad smile she usually wore. Here and there, she'd interrupt my babbling with, "It's fine, dear. I understand. You did the best you could. Maybe she'll just leave it alone now."

Later that night, well after bedtime, I tiptoed downstairs to get a drink. Mom and Dad were in the kitchen talking about my reaction to seeing Mom with the dress. I hid in the corner just behind the kitchen door and listened, knowing if they caught me, I'd be in huge trouble.

"But, Frank," my mother said, "You didn't see her. She was nearly hysterical. And how in the world could she possibly make that story up? How would she know about small pox? She's only in kindergarten. They don't teach history in kindergarten!"

"Maybe she heard it on the TV. I don't know. I know this, this house is not haunted. There's no such thing as ghosts."

"Well, I don't believe in it either, but nothing else makes sense. What about that name? You know as well as I do that previous owner's name was Bowman. How could she know that? We don't even know anyone named Margaret. How did she come up with that name?"

"Look, we can easily put an end to this nonsense. Just go to the clerk's office or the library and see what you can come up with. I'm betting you won't be able to find a Margaret Bowman connected with this house."

About that time my tummy rumbled and I gasped in fear. Before they could come looking for the cause of the noise, I quietly raced back upstairs.

The next morning I got up, got dressed, had breakfast, and went off to school as usual. Mom didn't say one word about Margie or the dress. When I came home that afternoon, she looked puzzled. During my afterschool snack, she asked me a few more questions about Margie, but never bothered to tell me why she wanted to know. That weekend we had our big Halloween party. Mom dressed as a zombie, but the torn up, paint spattered clothes she wore we her own.

As the weeks progressed, Mom's Margie questions became a snack time ritual. Christmas came and went, then Valentine's Day, and soon it was almost time for summer once again. Occasionally, way late at night, I'd hear Mom and Dad arguing about something. Inevitably, Margie's name would be mentioned, but as soon as it was, they'd start talking so softly, I couldn't hear anymore. My last day of kindergarten, I came home to find the living room full of half-packed boxes. I was devastated. We were moving to a new town. I would be going to a new school. And worst of all, I'd be leaving my beloved friend behind.

The day we left for the new house, I sat in the car looking up at our room. Margie stood in the window smiling her sad smile and waving goodbye. Tears rolled down my cheeks as my dad backed out of the driveway. He glanced back at me and said, "Now don't worry, baby. You'll have other friends. Lots of them, I promise!"

I wonder, now that I'm grown, if we would have moved had he known the absolute truth of his statement. I did make other friends. The kind everyone could see and the kind only I could see. But none of them were like my Margie.

STILL HAUNTED

PENNY JARS

In the annals of true ghost stories, this one probably will not rank high on the scale that grades how scary the encounter was. After all, my experience with the ghost and the penny jar was in a very familiar place, not a haunted mansion or otherwise scary location. Nope, my encounter was in my bedroom at the home of my grandmother and her parents; and the ghost was someone very familiar to me—my great-grandmother, Elizabeth.

First, let me backtrack a bit and give you a little history about my great-grandmother. My first memory of her was when I was just about five years old. She was a feisty lady in her late seventies at that time. And she was as crazy as a bed bug. The story goes that she was dropped on her head as a child and that caused her to have seizures periodically. I don't know about that, I never saw her have any when she was alive, and never saw any after she was gone. But she definitely liked to cause trouble; like a small precocious child she would always do the opposite of what she was told to do.

What I also remember about her was how small she was. The white hair piled on top of her head in a continually messy bun could not add any length to her petite 4'11" frame. But to my small eyes she was a giant. I also remember her as having a sharp tongue, and it was usually directed at my mom. She argued about everything with my mom, from how my mom should have made us drink all our milk at the bottom of the cereal bowl, to how we were not properly respectful children. She was all about being respectful and finishing what you start.

She smelled of tomatoes and sugar, her favorite snack. I would sit with her in the morning-- we were both morning people and often had breakfast hours before anyone else stirred in the mornings--and talk about anything that came to mind. My great-grandmother had left school before she finished the fifth grade and was not well educated, but she liked to read and we talked a lot about books. And she always encouraged me to read.

Something else that gave my great-grandmother supreme pleasure was to make my mom mad enough that she would argue with her. And my mom often rose to the bait. One of the reasons they fought was because of the Penny Jar.

Because we lived in Western NY, and my grandmother and her parents lived in New York City, we visited for holidays and possibly a week in the summers, if we were not traveling elsewhere. My parents were both teachers so had summers off and we traveled the country quite a bit. Getting to remain in one place for more than a day was a treat in the summers, so when we knew we were going to visit my mom's mom and grandparents we were always excited.

While the trips were fun for us kids--I have three siblings, two sisters and a brother--it was never fun for my mom. My great-grandmother was not nice to my mom and constantly criticized her. And she did not care when or where she did this, often picking fights in front of us kids, which embarrassed my mom. My mom's generation respected their elders so she would not fight back in front of us, but I am sure they had words after we left the room.

My grandmother would step in and try to prevent the battles, but she invariably lost the war. The battles raged on until my great-grandmother passed away.

But before she died one of her favorite tricks to upset my mom was to leave a treat for me each time we visited. For some reason she really took to me, perhaps because I was the first granddaughter, and she was trying to irritate my mom by stealing my affection?

The first morning that we were there I would wake up to a Mason jar or old mayonnaise jar filled to the brim with pennies. Old pennies, new pennies, shiny pennies, dirty pennies, pennies that had laid in the road and had chips and nicks in them, or pennies worn so smooth you could not read the date stamped on them.

Nothing but pennies.

And boy was I excited to get them! I would split them up into four piles and share with my sisters and brother (not by choice I assure you, I was between 7-10 for most of this and really wanted all the pennies for me) and off we would go to the candy store to fill up on penny candy. Well, my sisters and I would; my brother always saved his...I wasn't so smart.

After a few trips to NYC with the anticipated jars of pennies, my mom had a talk with my great-grandmother and told her that I was not to get any more jars. So my great-grandmother got sneaky and would hide them in my suitcase, or in my socks and say the gremlins had left them for me, or put them in my cereal bowl and pretend she had no idea how they got there.

Finally my mom gave up. And my great-grandmother could be heard snickering whenever we visited, like a little kid who had just stolen all the cookies and gotten away with it. She really was like a little kid. Probably why she and I got along so well. While I did not like the way she treated my mom, I was just a kid so what could I do? I just accepted the pennies and shared them with everyone else and whenever my great-grandmother would give them to me I would smile like we shared a deep dark secret. It became a game after a while.

A short while after the time my mom finally gave in to the inevitable, my great-grandmother passed away. Since we lived so far away only my mom attended the funeral. She brought me back a jar of pennies that my great-grandmother had left me in her will. This jar, with my mother's blessing, I did not split with my siblings. I actually kept it on my dresser for a long time before finally putting the money in the bank.

We were visiting my grandmother several months later and when I went up to my room I laid down on my bed to take a nap. I missed my great-grandmother a lot and couldn't believe she was gone. When I woke up for dinner I saw a jar on the dresser that I could have sworn was not there when I had come in. Neither of my sisters, with whom I shared the room, could remember having seen it there either.

It was, of course, full of pennies. I picked it up and looked around the room in confusion. I remember that I could faintly smell fresh cut tomatoes and sugar, the scents I remembered my great-grandmother always bringing into the room with her.

I know she was in the room with me.

I remember thanking her for the jar before setting it back on the dresser and going downstairs to see if anyone knew why it was there. I vaguely remember thinking that it might have been one that she had been collecting for me before she died and that they had missed it when my mom had brought me the other one after the funeral.

I asked everyone in the house: my grandmother, my great-uncles, my great-grandfather, my parents and siblings and none of them admitted to putting the jar there.

And so the tradition continued. Every time I visited I got a jar of pennies. At first I suspected my grandmother was keeping up her mother's tradition, but I knew she had agreed with my mom that there was no need for the jar of pennies, so I finally realized it was not her. And as I grew older I just accepted it as the norm. It did not frighten me; it was so nice of her. And I noticed all the penny dates stopped the year she died. I never got one penny that was newer than that year.

My last penny jar came the week I visited my grandmother, who was quite old now and ready for a nursing home. We were cleaning out her house as we prepared to move her out. I went to bed exhausted and sad because I would not be able to visit this house anymore after I left the next day.

On the dresser, in the morning when I woke up, was a jar.

But inside the jar, instead of hundreds of pennies, was a single penny. Shiny, brand new and resting on the bottom of the jar. It was a promise of new beginnings, and her final farewell.

To this day I cannot pass up a penny wherever I find one left lying around without remembering the Penny Jar and the love that my great-grandmother had for me.

Susan Burdorf was the winner of the Willow Cross True Ghost Story Contest. A very special thanks goes out to Susan for her lovely, heartwarming story.

Penny Jars Author Bio:

Susan Burdorf is a lover of anything paranormal. Affliction, book one of The Healer's Daughter series will release later this year. When not writing, Susan can be found in the company of her grandchildren or children making memories, which she hopes they save in jars like pennies...

HAUNTED IV

Prologue

This installment of Haunted, although told in first person, contains the paranormal encounters of a few of my friends. I am relaying the stories to you in the way they were told to me. Although some poetic license has been taking with wordage, nothing has been added for dramatic effect. As far as I know, the events which transpired in each story are true. I have no reason to believe otherwise.

~Willow Cross

BILL'S CHALLENGE

(This story was relayed to me by one of my facebook gamer friends. We've known each other quite some time and I have no reason to believe he would give me false information. I've attempted to rewrite his story keeping it as close as possible to his actual words.)
~Willow Cross

This is my story. Everything I am about to tell you is true. The names have been changed to protect the innocent, except for mine, because I could never be called innocent.

I was twenty-one and very full of myself. My girlfriend was drop dead gorgeous and I was totally smitten. Life was great! I had a good job, low rent, and great friends. And I was cocky, a little too cocky, as you will shortly find out.

Sandy, my girlfriend, had disappeared and her parents were very concerned and upset. We contacted everyone we thought she might contact, but no one had heard or seen her. After that, the police became involved.

Scared and heartbroken, I went to some mutual friends, Cindy and Steve, to cry the blues. They were great people, close friends. We talked long into the night and when I left, I was still upset, but I felt better.

Two weeks later, we found out she and a friend had taken off with a couple of guys they had met and were eight hundred miles away. I was relieved, crushed and very pissed. When you are a twenty-one year old male that is not a good combination, but when you add cocky into the mix it can go from bad to 'hold my beer and watch this shit' bad.

I went over to Cindy and Steve's place to give them the news. I suppose I should mention that at the time I was involved in the occult. Truth be told I was clueless. I was very into astral projection. Cindy had mentioned countless times she'd like to learn more about it and eventually wanted to try it. Being young and cocky, I didn't take into consideration my mental state that night. I was understandably not in the right frame of mind and was too distraught to concentrate on anything other than Sandy.

We sat and talked, they asked if I was ok, I lied and said I was just relieved. Once again, Cindy asked about astral projection and we decided to try it later in the evening. But things got weird, and I mean weird fast.

Around two pm Cindy felt a strong desire to use her Ouija board. I had never seen one. Oh, I knew about them, but no idea if they really worked, and I was intrigued.

She took out the board and we placed our hands on the planchette. After a few minutes, she looked up and said, "My spirit guide has a message for you. You need to be careful. You've pissed something off in the spirit world."

Before I could say anything, the planchette started moving again. From one letter to the next, the board spelled out LEAVE. The entity then told me to reproduce with myself, but not quite so politely.

Now if you remember, I stated I was cocky. What I failed to mention was that I was also rash and a little drunk. I announced I would meet this spirit on his turf. Yeah, I really did.

Eight hours later, much less drunk, sober really, Steve had gone upstairs to bed. Cindy and I decided to try a session with astral projection. I had already put the Ouija board incident out of my mind.

We laid down on the floor about a foot or so apart. I could feel the familiar shift in my body that signaled I was close.

To this day, thirty some odd years later, this still gives me goose bumps.

At first I only *heard* the tapping coming from the floor beneath me. Within a few seconds, not only was the sound audible, but I could feel the floor vibrate with each new tap. It followed the contour of my body in rapid succession. Faster and faster the tapping came, until it was a blur of sound and motion.

Simultaneously, Cindy and I sat straight up.

"Did you hear that shit?" I asked.

Wide eyed, she nodded. "Has that ever happened before?"

The look on my face answered her.

Cindy pulled out her Ouija board to get some answers. The board spelled out a direct warning to me to stop meddling with things that were not my concern. I don't know what I was really meddling with, but since then, I haven't dabbled in the occult in any way. The whole thing still freaks me out some. To the point that even now, while writing this down, I feel like I'm being watched.

HELL HOUSE

(This story was given to me by one of the dear folks on my fan page. She graciously consented to my infernal grilling in an attempt to acquire as much detail as humanly possible, as well as allowing me to share her story. I have no reason to believe anything she told me was less than an honest and truthful account of what transpired during her time in the Hell House.)

~Willow Cross

Our story started in 2004 in Muncie, Indiana. I was recovering from a serious illness and my husband had lost his job due to taking too much time off for my hospitalizations.

We found a church willing to donate a home to us for a few months. The situation was perfect. I could heal from my latest surgery without worrying about bills, and my husband would have plenty of time to find a job, so we could get back on our feet.

The house had been built in the 1800s and sat directly across the street from a cemetery also dating back to the late 1800s. The structure was a large two story with two upstairs windows over the porch. Honestly, except for the fact it was yellow, it reminded me of the famous Amityville house. The inside was beautiful; all dark wood paneling and hardwood floors throughout. Downstairs, there was a living room and bedroom off to the right with a small kitchen in the back of the house. Upstairs, were two bedrooms right across from each other and a bathroom in the middle with the most amazing claw footed tub I'd ever seen. No shower, but with an awesome tub like that, who needs a shower?

The kid's room had a huge walk in closet and the door to the attic was in there too. The other bedroom was small, closer to the size of a typical bathroom.

The first week or so went by quickly and without any trouble other than general unpacking issues. My husband even found a job working nights. Right away, we started a schedule where we'd bathe our four children, settle them in bed, and watch TV until he left for work.

One night, we'd just made it downstairs when my seven year-old daughter let out a horrific scream. We immediately raced back up the stairs to see what had happened, and found her nearly hysterical.

Stuttering through tears, she said, "The woman in the bathroom told me to get out. Sh-she said we aren't welcome here."

"What woman?" I asked.

"The old lady with the stick," she sobbed.

Of course, we figured it was just a nightmare, but after all her fussing, we agreed she could sleep in her brothers' room. After a while, she finally went back to sleep. From that point on, things went downhill rather quickly.

It began with things moving to unexpected places. Just stupid little things, keys mostly, but in addition to the disappearing/reappearing items, toys would turn on and off. My son had this fire truck that went off so much, we took the batteries out, and it would still go off. Eventually, we tore wires out, and it still went off. My purse disappeared and later, I found it upstairs in the tub. Change, medicine, and diapers were constantly moved somewhere strange. Places I knew I'd never have just sat them or tossed them.

And then there was the lighting situation. Lights would spontaneously turn on and off. All over the house. Doors opened or closed seemingly without anyone around to do it. We just blew it off, blaming it on the kids, or us not paying attention. But it always started when my husband left for work.

One night I was watching TV in bed and started hearing something moving around in the bedroom below mine. It was empty since my other daughter refused to sleep in it. It wasn't the greatest neighborhood, so as I headed down to investigate, I grabbed a baseball bat. As soon as I got downstairs I heard someone upstairs. Moving and talking and walking around. I ran right back up...and nothing. No one was there. The kids were asleep and the TV was muted.

Bewildered and a little freaked out, I stood in the hallway with my back to the bathroom door listening for intruders. Finally, I heard a board squeak behind me. Turning around, I stared straight into the face of a glaring old woman standing in the bathroom doorway. Her silver hair was pulled tightly into a bun, giving her a harsh appearance. Her blue flowered dress nearly matched her terrifying eyes. I will never forget those eyes. They were just so...dead. Redundant I know, but they held no compassion, no love, and no soul. The most hateful, angry eyes I have ever seen. In her right hand she held an ornately carved cane.

Raising her cane until it pointed directly at me, she said, "Leave."

Even now the appearance of that woman is scorched into my memory. Before I could even process what was going on, the bathroom door slammed and the light bulb above my head blew apart.

Now wide awake, the kids started screaming because it was pitch black, and rushed into the hall. We were all terrified.

As quickly as I could, I hustled them into my room and locked the door. I had no trouble staying awake until my husband got home. Each passing minute felt like an eternity.

When he finally made it into the house, I told him everything that had happened the night before. He listened, but I could tell the longer I went on, the angrier he was getting. By the time I was done, he was fully steamed.

His accusatory tone rolled over me like a wave. "You are just playing into the kid's lies!"

"I am not! Why would I say something like that if it wasn't true?"

"All this ghost crap you've been talking about has your imagination in overdrive. You're the adult here."

Now we didn't fight often. Almost never really. Not until we'd moved into that house. From day one there was something different about living there. Almost like a dark cloud of doom and gloom surrounded the place. It wasn't long before we were arguing as much as the children and with them, it was almost constantly.

The biggest fight occurred while I had my five year-old niece staying the weekend. My brother, who was fifteen at the time, was staying over too. By then we'd turned the attic attached to the childrens' room into a play area. All of the kids had gone in and had been playing quite some time before my brother and I heard their muffled yells and banging. When we went upstairs to investigate, we discovered the door to the attic was locked. It wasn't a bolt lock or anything intricate, just a plain old finger latch deal on the outside of the door. All of the kids were in the room and we'd been downstairs, so who locked the door? Try as we might, we couldn't get the latch to move. Something had jammed and it wasn't budging. We finally had to take the hinges off and remove the whole door to get them out.

After that, every night we were attacked in some way until we realized most of the activity was upstairs. Finally, we literally made a big bedroom in the living room and all six of us slept there. We only had the one bathroom, which was upstairs, so we had bathroom buddies. No one was to go up there alone. Ever.

One night I was running late with our schedule and hadn't gotten around to cleaning up the supper mess in the kitchen until much later than usual. I had just finished putting the dishes away when I went to change the twins' diapers. I was only in the other room for a few minutes, but when I went to throw the diapers away, every single dish was out of the cabinets. They were stacked on the counters, the kitchen table, even the floor. All the cabinets and drawers were standing open. I grabbed all the kids and drove to my husband's work. We slept in the parking lot.

Living there had become unbearable. I couldn't stand being in the house alone with the children. Every day I lived in constant fear of what might happen next. It got to the point that I spent weeks with my parents or would beg friends or family stay with me. When all else failed, we would sleep in the parking lot of my husband's workplace.

All this time, my husband refused to believe our stories. He'd never witnessed anything since he was always at work at night. And anytime we brought it up, or tried to discuss it with him, he'd instantly be angry. After weeks of arguments and dissent, he was sent home from work early. The kids and I were gone and for the first time ever, he was home alone.

According to him, he'd flipped the TV on, and went upstairs into the bathroom. While he was in there the door to the medicine cabinet swung open, and one by one, bottles flew off the shelves.

Freaked out, he headed toward the stairs, but as soon as his foot landed on the first step, he felt something behind him push hard. Losing his footing, he fell the rest of the way down. Days after the attack he still had two handprints on his back. Needless to say, after that he was no longer skeptic.

One would think that his abrupt change of heart would have helped the arguing situation. However, one would be dead wrong. Anger and desperation sent all of us on an emotional roller coaster and the fighting accelerated. We were stuck. Completely and totally imprisoned in a house of horrors. With such a big family, and even with his good job, we didn't have the money to just find a different house.

There was a constant barrage of shadow people,

and the old woman frequently made herself known. Ghostly footsteps could be heard any time. And with unexplainable scratching and bruising, I lived in terror of what these entities would do to my children.

We tried everything we could think of. We had the house blessed. Twice. It made it worse. I've never felt so hopelessly trapped in my entire life.

The night before my last surgery, we stayed at my husband's mother's house. I had to be at the hospital early, so it was just easier to stay there and not have to worry about the kids.

My husband went back to our house with his mom to pick up some things only to discover someone had robbed us. He called the police and while they were waiting for them to arrive, they sat on the living room couch. Toys, books, socks, all manner of things started lifting off the floor and flying into them as if someone was picking up anything they could find and throwing it. They escaped outside and had to wait there for the officers to come take the report.

After I got out of the hospital, my husband and I went back to the house to meet with members of our church. They had secretly taken up a collection for our family and gave us the check. Thankfully, it was enough to get us out of that hell. We didn't take anything with us when we left. We didn't want to take a chance that anything tainted with the evil in that place would follow us to our new home.

These are just a few of the stories about the paranormal events that occurred in that wicked place. There were so many more things that happened to us, along with other people's stories who also lived there. No one lasted as long as we did. We made it six months. Truly the most terrifying time in our lives, it left

us with scars that still haven't healed. I'm still hoping
that some day they will.

THE CLOSET MONSTER

(This story came from a good friend of mine. As this happened when he was very young, some of the finite details have been lost. Should you find gaps in the story, it is only due to memory loss and time lapse, which is completely understandable considering thirty some years have passed since the actual event.)

~Willow Cross

I was nine when it happened. Well, when it started. We had just moved from Missouri to Arkansas to stay with my Grandmother, who was an extremely devout Christian woman. You wouldn't think that should make a difference in a story like mine, but it does. You'll understand why later.

Many things about the events that took place have been lost to the passage of time. Strangely though, certain things are still so fresh in my mind I can close my eyes and I'm there again. Like the smell of the sheets. I clearly remember the smell of the sheets and pillow case of the bed in which I was lying. Funny how after all these years, I can still remember the different smells in her house.

My little sister and I were sharing the spare room, just off the living room, right beside the kitchen. We had to share a full sized bed, and a dresser. The bed faced the wall adjacent to the kitchen and sat directly in the center of the opposing wall, right in front of the closet door.

After dinner, we bathed, put our pajamas on, and Grandma had dropped in to tuck my little sister and myself in bed. Neither of us were frightened of the dark, nor were we scared to sleep in our little room at Grandma's house. As we were quite comfortable, we settled in quickly and shortly fell asleep.

I remember I'd been dreaming about something, but I can't tell you now what that something was. I do, however, remember being irritated to be woken up. Both the closet door and the main bedroom door creaked loudly when opened and closed. So when I heard that loud squeaking begin, I sat up in bed and looked around. I was expecting to see my mother at the main door, but that door was still closed.

My eyes immediately locked on the now partially open closet door. Even though the lights were out, the room wasn't pitch black. The outside security light let in more than enough light to see clearly. The squeaking sound came again and the closet door opened a little more.

Confused, but still not afraid, I just kept staring at the door trying to figure out why it was moving. Then I heard another sound. It wasn't really a growl, not like a dog, or an animal sound, but I don't have a better word for it. I will never forget that sound, and to date, I haven't heard anything remotely like it.

Now as crazy as this sounds, even though I know this all happened in a matter of seconds, it felt like minutes were passing, as if time had somehow slowed down to a snail's pace. Long, skeletal fingers slipped around the top of the closet door. The claw-like hands were covered in yellowish skin that didn't quite look like skin, and tipped with long, jagged fingernails. Suddenly I was unable to move. Frozen in place, with my heart racing, I felt my mouth open to scream, but no sound was coming out.

When the door finally reached the half-way mark, the creature inside pushed its head out of the closet. The thing was so tall it looked like it was hunching over. And it's face, good God I will never forget that face either! It had waist-length, bright red hair and a matching goatee that hung way down past where its chest should have been. The same yellowish skin covered its sunken cheeks, highlighting dark holes where its eyes should have been. The nose was thin and stretched down the face like something you'd see in an old horror comic.

The creature's thin lips parted, showing razor sharp teeth and it growled again. Bright red pulsating light appeared in the dark hollow eyes and then...I heard screaming. A high pitched, ear-splitting scream, coming from right beside me. Finally able to move, I looked over at my little sister who was sitting beside me screaming her head off. Time sped back up and my Grandma came bursting through the bedroom door, carrying her bible and praying loudly.

The creature was gone. Only an open closet door remained to show it had ever been there. My mother swooped in right behind Grandma and ushered us out of the room. Grandma spent a long time in there after we'd been put to bed in the living room. Hours later, I could still hear her intermittently praying and crying, or reading from the bible.

Not much was ever said about that room or what happened that night. My little sister, to this day, will not even speak of it. When I was in my early twenties I had a talk with Grandma about that night and what happened there. She told me that there had always been something dark in that house. She had no idea where it came from, but it seemed to stay just in that room. Several times, people from her church had come over to bless the house, but finally they'd given up, sold it, and moved out. I drove by about three months after they'd sold it and the house was gone. Completely gone. No slab underneath still showing, no debris, just a completely empty lot full of grass.

Just a year or two ago, I attended a civil war festival being held in the lot where Grandma's house used to be, and ran into a local historian. I didn't tell her who I was, we just chatted about the town's history. She claimed that from way back to the time the land in our area was populated by the local Indian tribes, there had been talk about the land being tainted by something evil that had been buried somewhere in the area. I'm pretty sure it's somewhere on that property.

FOLLOWING DEATH

(This particular story was given to me by an old high school chum. Although she willingly shared her story, she vehemently requested I keep her name secret. Although this happened many years ago, she said she's only told this to a handful of people. Even now she worries people will believe she's crazy.)

~Willow Cross

The one and only paranormal event I've ever encountered happened in 1985. It was late fall during my senior year of high school. One of my friends, who lived way out in the country outside of Uniondale, Indiana, had hosted a kegger after a football game. I remember it was an unusually warm October night. More times than not, you need warm jackets and blankets at a football game, but not this night.

By the time I arrived at the party, it looked like half the school was there. There were cars parked all over the front yard and even some in the field next to the house. Kids were milling around a gigantic bonfire just talking and laughing. You know, the things we normally did at parties. The 'rowdies' were already hard at it over by the kegs doing beer bongs and keg stands.

I don't know why I didn't feel like drinking that night. Back then, I partied like a rock star, but that night...I just didn't have it in me. About midnight the temperature started to drop and a chill set in bringing fog with it. The fog was really strange. It was almost like a TV show the way it came in. Or maybe like something you'd see at a lake. It came from the east, rolling in across the open field like an ocean wave. Most of the party goers got a big kick out of it. Some were making references to the movie 'The Fog,' and the guys were trying to freak all the girls out. But it bothered me. I mean it really unnerved me. Something felt terribly wrong about that fog. About the whole night really.

Now I'm not psychic. I've never claimed to be and I've never really had any other experience, other than the occasional bout of déjà vu, that would even remotely lead me to believe I had an ability of that nature. However, I could not get the sensation of 'wrongness' to go away. I tried to put it out of my mind, but it was firmly planted, and there was nothing I could do about it.

I stayed for another hour, but the drunker my friends got, the less fun I had, so I finally decided to head on home. As I got into my car and backed out of the driveway, a cold chill ran down my back. I didn't think much of it; I just leaned forward and flipped on the heater.

I turned on 116 and headed towards Bluffton. Just before Murray, there's a deep curve in the road. I was already only driving about 30 mph due to the fog, so when I came up behind a horse drawn carriage going even slower, I was pissed. I was already late for my curfew and this would slow me down even more.

Thinking back now, the fact that a carriage was going down the road at one AM should have spooked me a bit. We are very close to Amish country in that area, so seeing horses pulling buggies is quite normal. However, this most definitely wasn't a buggy. It was very large, covered in what looked like black fabric, and had fancy tassels hanging from the top corners. Four incredibly tall, black horses with thick, silky manes were pulling it, not the standard one or two we'd normally see.

When we finally made it around the bend, I decided to ignore the double yellow lines and pass the thing. Carefully watching for oncoming traffic, I sped up beside it and looked over. The driver was wearing a black hooded cloak that covered everything except his hands.

It all happened so fast that I can't help but wonder if my mind was playing tricks on me, or if I really saw what I saw. The hands weren't hands. They were bones. No skin, no muscle, just bones. It scared me so bad, I floored the gas pedal and pulled back into the lane in front of it.

I immediately looked into my rearview mirror to see if I could still make out the details of those hands, or possibly get a better look at the driver. It was gone. There's no way enough time could have passed for it to have pulled off the road and I wasn't that far ahead of it. It was just gone.

I don't know what I saw on the road that night, but I know I don't ever want to see it again.

THE HOUSE EVIL BUILT

(This story was relayed to me from another online friend. Due to the events that took place in her house, she's done extensive research into the occult and is quite the paranormal aficionado. She has asked me to be very clear when re-telling her story, and make sure that you, as readers, understand that if your heart is telling you to get out...you do so. There are no good reasons to stay somewhere potentially dangerous.)

~Willow Cross

In March of 2005, my family hit a very rough spot. I'd been a stay at home mom for six years, and my husband, our sole provider, had been injured in a car wreck on his way home from work. Due to his extended stay in the hospital, multiple surgeries leaving us with a mountain of medical bills, and the loss of his income, we found ourselves on the brink of homelessness.

We'd done everything we could. I managed to find a full time job working at a fast food joint, and my mother watched the children who weren't still in school, but with so many extra expenses, we just couldn't manage to keep up on our house payment.

I'd spent two weeks combing through newspapers and searching online for a rental place close enough to where I worked and mom lived, before I finally found a place out in the country. It really was a bit too far from mom's house, but the rent was only $350 a month. Honestly, I figured it had to be a dump, but beggars can't be choosy and we were most certainly about to be begging.

After contacting the landlord, we drove out to the house to meet him. The two-story house sat back a long driveway that wound through two acres of woods. The old white paint was peeling in huge chunks all over and the small front yard was overgrown with weeds and grass. It had large windows all across the front, six in all, and the rickety front porch looked exactly like what I'd expected to see. But it had potential. In my mind's eye I could see how charming and quaint the old house would look with a couple coats of pain and some yard work.

I got out of the car and walked over to Mr. Hodges, the landlord. He looked nervous and fidgety, and I assumed it was because the place was in such a state of disrepair.

"Good morning!" I said, trying to ease him a bit. I began to hope that his obvious distress might allow me to haggle for a lower rent rate.

"Mrs. Evens?" He answered.

When I nodded, he abruptly thrust the keys into my hands, saying, "Go have a look. Take care on the porch, some of those boards are rotted through." And without another word, he got right back into his car and closed the door.

Honestly, I was pretty irritated. I mean seriously, this guy didn't care enough about his rental property to even walk me through it? What the hell?

I tentatively stepped on the first of three stairs leading to the porch and looked back at Mr. Hodges. He was on his cell gabbing away and wasn't even looking in my direction. Sighing, I carefully walked up the steps and almost tiptoed across the porch to the front door. It had a large, oval, dirt-covered window in the center of it, with a dingy lace curtain hanging inside.

Looking down at the key chain, I chose one of the two keys on it and attempted to unlock the door. Of course, it was the wrong key, so I tried the other one. That time it slid right in the lock, so I twisted the key, and opened the door.

As the door opened, a cool, stale gust of air swooshed over me. It was really weird. Taken aback, once again I looked back at the landlord. This time his eyes were intently focused on me. He had an expression on his face akin to anticipation, but not quite. Dread, maybe? While I watched him, he leaned forward in the car seat like he was trying to get a better look. *What a freaking nut job,* I thought.

Looking back at the house, I decided my best course of action would be to ignore him and just get this over with. I stepped into a long hallway. To my right, was a door at the bottom of a stairway. Further up ahead on the left was an entry way to what I figured would be the living room, and at the far end of the hall I could see a linoleum floor and part of a kitchen table with a chair.

I took a deep breath, and moved inside to investigate the bottom floor. As I'd suspected, the living room was through the left entryway. I was really surprised to see the entire room was not only furnished, but filthy as well. A large sofa with matching love seat and chair were centered around a decent sized TV. One of those old console floor models they don't sell any more. The walls were covered in someone's family pictures and crucifixes. Lots of both. Blankets and clothing were strewn about the room like someone had just had a sleepover with a multitude of children. If it hadn't been for the thick layer of dust covering everything, I would have thought someone still lived here.

The kitchen was in about the same state, only worse. The cupboard doors were hanging open, broken dishes lay on the floors and counters, and both sides of the sink were filled with dirty dishes. There was even rotting food in the refrigerator. I couldn't help but wonder if the landlord was such an ass that he threw the last tenants out without even allowing them to get their things. People don't just up and leave all their stuff behind. Do they?

Upstairs, the three bedrooms were in various stages of dishevelment. All of them fully equipped with beds, dressers, decor, and the previous tenant's personal items. The smallest room obviously had been used as a nursery as it still held a baby bed, changing table, and a multitude of toys. It was by far one of the craziest things I'd ever seen. And creepy. It was really creepy to be walking around in a house full of other people's stuff.

Except for the debris and dirt, the inside of the house wasn't that bad. It would take a lot of cleaning and God knows how many trips to the dump to get rid of all this stuff, but for $350.00 a month, it was a good deal. All the rooms except the kitchen had hardwood floors. The upstairs bathroom had a tub/shower combo. The downstairs bathroom, just off the kitchen had just a toilet and sink. All in all it was a decent place for the money.

Carefully making my way back off the porch, I walked up to Mr. Hodges' car. Although he saw me coming, he didn't bother to do anything other than roll his window down.

"So what do you think?" he asked.

Trying to play it cool, I shrugged. "It's not in too bad of shape, but what are you going to do with all the stuff inside?"

He shook his head. "Nothing. It comes with the place, keep it, or throw it away if you don't want it."

I crossed my arms over my chest and sighed. "I don't want all that crap, and the place is filthy. It will take at least a week to clean it all out and get it ready to move my family in."

"If you're going to pay today, I don't care when you move in." He replied.

Just as I was about to lose my temper and walk away, he seemed to finally get my drift and spoke again. "Why don't we do this? Since you'll obviously have so much work to do, I'll drop the deposit and you can move in for just this month's rent."

An avid haggler, I took the opportunity to move in for the kill. "I'll tell you what, Mr. Hodges. My husband can't help with any of the moving or cleaning and the kids are too small, so all of that clean up will be on me. I can't afford to take off work for a week to get this place ready for us. How about I pay you next month's rent, no deposit, and we can move in as soon as I finally get it cleared out. Deal?"

His face turned red for a moment, but quickly

cleared away. His voice, however, was a bit disgruntled when he replied, "Fine."

I offered him my hand to shake and he just looked at it like I was diseased or something. Sighing, I reached in my purse, pulled out the right amount of money, and handed it to him.

He counted it three times before finally looking up at me with a grin. "Pleasure doing business with you, Mrs. Evens." Then, without so much as a see you when rent's due, or a goodbye, he rolled up his window, started his car, and backed out of the driveway.

I just stood there for a few moments watching him leave and wondering what in the hell was wrong with the man. Taking one last look at the house, I got in my car and headed home. I was dreading the work I was going to have to do, but I was very proud of myself for getting such a good deal. If I had known then what I know now, I would have chased him down and made him give my money back.

As soon as I arrived home, I called my mom to give her the good news. She in turn called her sisters and by 10pm that night we had a total of twelve family members willing to show up the next day and help out. Between the twelve of them, we would also have four trucks available. Now unlike most stories you hear about hauntings, there was no 'grace' period of settling in before the shit hit the fan. It would have been nice, but it started that very next day within fifteen minutes of the time everyone arrived to clean out the house.

We had seven men and six women show up. The women each took a room and were throwing stuff in garbage bags. We decided that instead of throwing everything away, we'd keep the usable stuff to sell in a garage sale later that summer. While the women were packing up, the men were hauling all the old furniture to the trucks to go to the dump.

My cousin Amy, who had just started working in the former nursery, rushed into what was going to be the master bedroom, obviously scared to death. Her eyes were wide and teary, and her face was almost completely white. "You can't live here!" she said.

"What? What's wrong with you?" I answered.

"This house is haunted. I mean like serious ghost hunter bullshit, dude. I was just filling a bag and I swear I heard a baby giggle. I looked around and something grabbed my leg and clung to it like a child would."

I couldn't help it, I started laughing. "You watch way too much TV, Amy. This house isn't haunted."

"It is. I swear it is. Just think about it. Why would anyone leave all their shit behind? People only do that when they are running from something! This house is haunted!"

Before I could answer, the door to the room she just vacated slammed loudly. My eyes moved from her, to the door across the hallway a couple of times.

"See?" she said.

Shaking my head, I brushed past her and went to the closed door. Turning the handle, I totally expected to see her husband Jake standing in there smirking. No one was there. The bag was still lying where she'd dropped it.

Feeling her walk up behind me, I turned to face her. "Your imagination is working overtime, girl. It was just the wind."

Her head moved side to side as she pointed over my shoulder. "Those were in the bag. I'd just put them in the bag right before I head the giggle."

Turning back around I looked to see what she was talking about. "What was in the bag?"

"Those stuffed animals on the shelf. I swear to God, every last one of them was in that trash bag."

Now I'm not a skeptic. I never have been. I believed in ghosts and hauntings, even though I'd never experienced anything of that nature. So at that point, I believed what she'd told me. However, I wasn't all that concerned about living with the ghost of a small child who was attached to his or her stuffed animals. I mean really...it's a baby. How bad can that be?

I patted her on the shoulder and told her it was all right. After all, a little Casper couldn't possibly be that much trouble. Trying to placate her, I sent her downstairs to help in the kitchen and I took over the cleanup in the room.

I hadn't been in there long, when I heard a man yell and loud thumps going down the stairs. Racing to the stairway, I saw my brother David lying at the bottom of the stairs. Everyone downstairs was either standing close helping him up, and those of us upstairs were standing at the top of the stairs. All of us were upset and asking if he was okay.

He got up slowly without speaking and looked up towards those of us at the top of the stairs. His face was almost ashen. "David, are you okay or not?" I asked.

He shook his head and shoved through the people below to go outside. We all filed out behind him.

When I got outside I saw him sitting on the tailgate of Jake's truck, drinking a bottle of water. We were all standing in a semi-circle around him, waiting to see if he'd speak and was okay. After drinking half the bottle, he wiped the sweat from his forehead and said,

"Someone pushed me down the stairs."

"What do you mean pushed you? You were completely alone!" My cousin Adam stated.

David shook his head. "I'm telling you, someone with huge hands hit the back of my shoulders and pushed me down the stairs. I felt it. Hell, I still feel it."

Sally, David's wife, maneuvered herself behind him and pulled his shirt back. Her eyes looked stricken as she looked up at me. "You better come see this." Then seemingly thinking better of it, she tapped his right arm. "Put your arms up. Let's take your shirt off."

"Why?" David asked.

"Just do it!" She answered.

He stood and pulled off his t-shirt.

"Now turn around," Sally said.

David turned his back to us and all up and down his back were dark bruises and scratches. At the top of his shoulders, one on each side, were deep bruises in the shape of hands. Big hands.

Everyone there gasped, some cussed, and a couple of my female cousins started crying.

I looked at Amy and found her staring at me. "You can't live here," she said.

Before I could respond, a resounding boom came from the house, as if every door in the house had simultaneously slammed. All of us turned to face the house. The front door that had been standing wide open was tightly shut. We were all scared, even the guys.

David shook his head and looked me in the eyes. "What are you going to do, Sis? Are we still cleaning it out?"

Devastated at the loss of an affordable home, and scared out of my mind, I shook my head. "I can't bring my kids here. It's not safe."

"I don't think it's safe for any of us to even be here cleaning right now," Sally said.

"What are we going to do with all this crap?" Amy asked.

We discussed it for a minute or two and decided to just pile it in the front yard. Thankfully the only things we'd left in the house were the boxes of garbage bags, and a butt load of cleaning supplies. We left it all there, every last thing. None of us wanted to step foot in that house again.

I stuck the keys in the mailbox and the last glimpse I got of that house was in my rearview mirror. The huge pile of furniture mixed with full garbage bags partially concealed my view of the front door, but not completely. Even from where I was in the driveway, I could see it was standing wide open again. No one had gone near that door. No one. We dumped all the crap on the ground, got in our vehicles, and left.

As soon as I got home, I called Mr. Hodges and told him we would not be moving in. He didn't even bother to ask why. When I asked for my money back, he hung up on me and that was the end of that. I couldn't afford to take him to small claims court and he knew it.

Our family ended up moving in with my mother. All of us crammed in her tiny little three-bedroom house for nearly five months before my husband was able to return to work and get us back on our feet. In that time, I spent several days at the library combing through old records and microfiche looking for answers about what happened in that house. It took almost two years before I finally pieced together the following information. And much of it came *after* I ran across an article in the newspaper about the house burning to the ground.

The house had burned completely to the ground three times. The first time was in 1860 when the original owner had killed his entire family of seven, set the house on fire, and hung himself from the rafters of a barn that was no longer there. After the horrible event, the property sat empty until 1923 when it was purchased by another family and a new house was built. That house burned to the ground four years later, killing the mother and twin two year olds. Once again the land sat empty until purchased by the Hodges family in 1955.

With a little more digging into the matter, now that I knew what to look for, I discovered that the Hodges family only lived in their shiny new house for six months. Relatively well off, they moved into town and had rented the house out ever since. When old man Hodges died in 1996, his son, my almost landlord, inherited the property. He had attempted to live there himself, but within three months of taking over his inheritance, he put the house on the market and tried to sell it.

According to the farmer whose property is adjacent to the old house, people came and went fairly frequently in that house. No one ever stayed more than a month or two. He'd stated that he and his wife had given up even trying to get to know the new neighbors because it became apparent the house was unlivable.

When I asked him if he thought the place was haunted, he glared at me, told me to have a good day, and walked away.

Other Books by Willow Cross

Haunted
Haunted II
Haunted III
Haunted IV
Haunted Special Combined Print Edition

Ghost Diaries
Case #1 The Haunting of Sarah Beth Hawkins
Case #2 The Haunting of Reginald Bonner
Case #3 The Unusual Evolution of Timothy Hicks

The Dark Gifts Series:
Birthright
Inheritance
Legacy (coming soon)

Dark Gifts Companions
Afterlife
The Bloodstone Oracle
Sacrifice (coming soon)

Oceans of Red Series
Volume one- Rise of the Demons
Volume two- Demon Evolution
Volume three- Demon Apocalypse

Oceans of Red combined print edition
Demon Revolution

**A Higher Calling
A Christmas Miracle**
~***~

ABOUT THE AUTHOR

Author Willow Cross has many published works in the paranormal genre including the Oceans of Red Series which is currently in the pre-production stages of filming for an online web series. In addition to writing, Willow moonlights as a radio talk show host on The Paranormal Hour for Blog Talk Radio's World of Ink Network, and is the founder of Willow's Indie Book Services, a continuously growing list of reputable professionals who provide a wide variety of publishing services for Indie authors.

Willow is a self-proclaimed vamp enthusiast, were-hunter, prankster, dreamer, story teller, benevolent dictator of minions, and chocolate lover. She resides in Arkansas with two children still young enough to live at home, an enormous cat named Bitsy, and a neurotic dog named Tank.

Her home has been known to host the occasional ghost, and although she dearly loves Vampires and Werewolves, they are never invited for dinner.

Made in the USA
Lexington, KY
18 July 2017